Tessa.Eh

Unheard, But Felt
The silent whisper of us

Tessa.Eh

Unheard, But Felt

Poetry

Impressum

Bibliografische Information der Deutschen Nationalbibliothek:
Die Deutsche Nationalbibliothek verzeichnet diese Publikation in der Deutschen Nationalbibliografie; detaillierte bibliografische Daten sind im Internet über http://dnb.dnb.de abrufbar.

Die automatisierte Analyse des Werkes, um daraus Informationen insbesondere über Muster, Trends und Korrelationen gemäß §44b UrhG („Text und Data Mining") zu gewinnen, ist untersagt.

© 2025 silentwhisperofme, Tessa.Eh

Lektorat: Tessa.Eh

Verlag: BoD · Books on Demand GmbH, Überseering 33, 22297 Hamburg, bod@bod.de

Druck: Libri Plureos GmbH, Friedensallee 273, 22763 Hamburg

ISBN: 978-3-7693-9825-0

A girl who writes because all of her friends do not like what she feels.

I know it is better for me to write about all the complicated things in my head.

I think that a lot of hearts felt the same hurt that I felt.

I hope you know that you are NOT alone.

I hope you have a lot of warming feelings while reading this book.

On every opposite page is a question or task to make this book a part of your own journey of healing.

I hope that when you read this book you let your feelings get loud, cry loud, sing or scream your hurt out, feel the hurt and know the worth of it, because even when you are still hurt and the healing is not linear, you are able to be happy and thankfull at the same time.

You are worth to be happy alone and with others.

You are worth all the things you give for others.

YOU ARE WORTH IT!

My Prayer for him

Please God,
help him to find his way back.
Back to his patient self.

You are the only reason,
you are the only person,
the only one who can heal him.
Heal us.

There are things he don´t talk about.
So please show him,
your strength&kindness.

And when there will be a right time,
for him and I to come back,
be by our sides and show us
how to treat each other right.

What would you pray for them?

Write it in the heart.

Autumn

The season of new beginnings.
The season that gave me, you.

In November, one day before my birthday our love began to
bloom.

With every cold, rainy day,
we found a love that seemed to stay.

Yet two years rolled on,
seasons turned and the flame that sparked began to burn.

What started pure in November ´22 cozy nights, faded in
a invincible fire that I could no longer extinguish alone.

A fire so bright, I couldn´t find you anymore.

Now November returns with bittersweet,
memories of love once so complete.

Though times has taken what we knew,
November still whispers „I loved you.“
But then the seasons changed.

Write down a memory this poem reminds you of.

____

____

____

____

____

____

____

____

____

____

____

____

____

____

Place for your little pictures:

Scared of the „again"

And sometimes we fall,
we are so hurt,
that we don´t dare anymore,
to open our eyes again.

Describe or draw your emotions about this poem:

Friends with benefits.

We are more than friends,
Exs with memories.
Memories made from gold and love.

But we are less than a couple.

We are two teenagers who don't want to grow up,
as long as one of us catches feelings again.

What question would you ask the poet about this writing?

Thoughts of 08´October´24

You were the most
 unrealistic and realistic thing
 that I ever experienced as far.

And nothing,
can ever,
change the fact that you are
the specialist person who ever was a part
of my entire life

In Love, Theresa

Your thoughts of _________:

Because of the touch of our souls

I love you

But I don´t love you now.
I love the „you" you were
when we were together.

The memories with you
still stuck in my heart.
they are engraved with
a thin fether of your love.

And yes…I still have it…

…the wierd feeling in my stomach.
But for now it is not because
I am so in love with you or with us.

It is because of our time.

\#

Write a letter to the person in this poem.

11 October '24- No words needed

And then you go home
And so do I
As if we don't need each other.

You wave and so do I.

For a moment you look like
You never fell asleep
Next to me

As if we never gone home together.

If this poem had a hidden message, what would it be?

FOR AN BLINK OF AN EYE

I saw it again
My eyes are closed
And all I saw
Was him
For an blink of an eye
I just saw his eyes
And how they once looked in mine
My heart felt paperthin

But just for an blink of an eye.

Write your own short poem inspired by this one.

Reveal

Your pulse reveals
How you are feeling
Even if you are silent.

It says more than
A thousands words.

It holds all our secrets in it.
Incredible how our heart tells us
how we really feel.

Sometimes more than we could ever imagine.

What are your thoughts about this poem?

25

I don´t want you to leave yet

The first fifth of November without you
The fifth of November
The day of our first kiss
The kiss of our beginning

It´s been two years now
Two years, two years ago today we were standing in your room
After we looked cars on disney.

I was with you for the first time
It was time for me to go home,
so we stood there,
hugging each other and looking into each others eyes.

My pulse escalated and I felt your lips on mine after you looked
in my eyes like enternity and said:

„I don´t want you to leave yet"

And these words are engraved on my heart.
It whispers „I don´t want you to leave yet"

Write about your first.....without them.

Maybe even more

Maybe I am,
maybe I am the writer of
our love and souls.

And yeah maybe I am the writer of
everything,
everything between us.

But at one point you can be sure,
you will always be a part of me and

the muse for the words of my writings.

Create a collage that match the poem´s theme:

Universes

Maybe in another universe…
But I still hope,
it happen in this.

Draw your own little univers.

YEARS AFTER BREAKING UP

It took them three years.
Three years until they met again.
Met again after breaking up.

First love gets a second chance.

What do you think about meeting someone twice?

In 2027?

It says that when two souls are not in connection with each other, you don´t meet them anymore.

But what is it?

We are not 100% seperrated. We doesn´t broken up because of toxic traits or even because we don´t love each other anymore.

Simply our lifes has changed and we had to choose other ways for a while. So we ended with the words:

„Maybe in three years…"

So please tell me,
will we try again in 2027?

Illustrate an allternative version of this poem

A thin wall between our silent
love and feelings…

We still write each other messages.
On my birthday you called me,
we talked for over an hour.

So there is still a kind of love between us,
a other kind of it,
the kind we don't talk about.

We just feel it through a thin wall.
You can hear that there is something,
 but you can't describe it.

Your free creative space:

Was it stupid to love you?

No.
It was the best thing that I ever experienced as far.
You are one of my golden memories&
in my eyes you are incredible.

But in poems we say:

„Honey all of the city lights
and all the coulors of the sunset,
will never be able to shine as bright as your eyes.“

What does this poem NOT say that you think it implies?

Under all the stars that fall down the sky

And under all the lights,
under all the candles,
stars and fireworks.

I saw it again.
Our love.

With every wave of the ocean,
every piece of mirrors
and every blue, little reflection,
I simply saw you.

Do you know the „pink-glasses" effect?

Bad decisions

42

I saw that video that says   „Let´s make one last bad decision
                                 before the year comes to an end.“

And I saw that you liked that reel.
But now there is a question in my head…
Do you ever thought that I was a bad desicion?
Or our break up?
Do you EVER thought that?

And these thoughts destroyed me.

Love is never a bad desicion.
Write your personal definition of true love at a young age.

There is no glimpse of us anymore.

My heart races, a frantic drum.
Cold shadows claim where warmth won't come.
Trembling hands, a silent cry.
You vanished- no reason
                    -no goodbye.

Yesterday, your touch was near.
Today, the void is all I hear.

How do I accept the sudden fall,
when love pretends it felt nothing at all?

What do you feel when you read this words?

The weight of silence

Silence is heavy,
        yet unseen.
A space between
where hearts convene.
Unspoken truths, a quiet pain.
Echos fall, but none remain.

What law of nature does this poem remind you?

I can´t catch these butterflys again.

Fear wraps my heart,
a cage of stone.
A place where love once brightly shone.
The shadows whisper, cold and near,
„You are too broken now to hold love dear.“

I reach for warmth, but find in the air,
an empty promise and no one there.
Can love return to this hallow space?
Or is it lost, without a trace?

What animal could symbolize your feelings about this feeling?

Scared to forget

I hear your voice, i am scared to forget it.
So I will keep your chats, each word you´ve set in it.
A fragile thread that ties me tight,
to memories fading into the night.

The laughter we shared, the pain we knew,
all locked in lines I scroll back through.
For if I lose this, what remains?
Only silence, and lingering pains.

So here I stand, in this fragile space,
a shadowed echo of your grace.
Your voice, your words- they anchor me
to love I fear I´ll never see again.

What happens in the world of this poem right after it ends?

The bells will chime, the year will turn
But my heart resists, my soul does burn.
Twelve months split in joy and pain.
Love once bloomed, then came the rain.
Hope flickerd dim,
yet trough it all,
I learned to rise, though I did fall.

The year took me much, yet gave me this:

A love for myself I won't dismiss.

Write a letter to your younger self about this….

A Gut Instinct

„She is just a friend", his words were plain.
But in my gut, I felt the strain.
Then came her message, sharp and bold,
her accusations took their hold.

„With you, he cheated, lied to me."
Her words cut deep, relentlessly.
She sents me chats, his words were clear.
The man I knew now seemed unclear.

I blocked her out, her voice too loud:
„Not a girls girl", she threw my way,
but I owed her nothing to this day.

I asked him to meet, for clarity,
but he replied, „Today, I can´t be free."
And so I stood, left to reflect,
unsure of what would happen next.

What are your experiences with the Gut Instinct?

The flowers decision´s

I told myself, „No more replies.“
Let silence fall, no last goodbyes.
But then the doorbell broke my thought,
a boquet there,my heart was caught.

My favorite blooms, so soft, so bright,
with babys breath, a gentle sight.
A card enclosed, a pink heart ballon,
„Let´s start again", it hummed a tune.

No name was signed, but I just knew,
only he would send this view.
He knew the flowers I adored,
but now I stand, unsure, ignored.

The year began with questions near.
And now I´m left with doubt and fear.
Flowers in hand,
but what´s my move?

To forgive or not-I must choose.

Draw your favorite flowers and what you associated with them.

Between

I don´t know what I want to feel.
Or if I still not healed.

I don´t even know what I´ll choose,
to forgive or not, I am so confused.

My head tells me to let him explain his view.
But will it be something new?

My heart doesn´t want to get that thin again.
So here I am, standing between them.

What is your „Between"?

Highs and Lows

Through all of my lows.
I am not alone,
I have a home.

I don´t have a mister, but you know what I have?
I have a sister.

I cried for days because of a boy who crahes into my soft,
worthy heart.

She tells me, „He isn´t good enough and he don´t know what
he´s doing there…“
And even when I would go back to him for a thousand times,
she will always be by my side.

Even when I am not fair to her.
She is ALWAYS there.
Through all of the lows and all the highs,
she will always be by my side.

I Love You.

Draw a line with all of your last highs and lows:

Write a little note to the one person who was there for you in your highs and low.

____

____

____

____

____

____

____

____

____

____

What I need to feel good…

A warm hug, more than just a second.

Sun kissed skin, kissed like him.

A happy and free mind,
exactly like I saw his, very kind.

A night filled with love and laughter,
like my heart never hurted.

Trust into good people,
where I can fall with closed eyes.

What do you need to feel good?

63

What do you need to feel good?

Double standards

You talk bad about him
                    while you don´t even treat me better.
I say that I don´t hate him,
and that for my inner peace.
                        You only hear that I am still attached.
                        You say I deserve better.
Then you leave me out of it.
                        You say that you want the best for me,
the next second
you don´t stand beside me.
                     You are my friends, yes.
                     But don´t act like you are better than him,
                     don´t act like you know me better.

When the wave reaches the beach, I stand there alone in the
current.

Write one word per line to describe how this poem makes you feel.

The one I thought is gentle

The one I thought would never be mean to me.
Sat in silence, let them speak.
I wasn´t there, I didn´t hear,
but whispers found their way to me.

She laughed, she lied, she tries to tore me down.
Called me „fake", spun my name around.

She doesn´t know me, but you, I thought you know me.
I thought I know you.

But you sat there, a quiet „hm",
no word, no shield, no fight for me.

It wasn´t her that cut me deep,
not her false words, not what she speaks.
But you- your silence, loud and near.
The one I thought I trusted nowhere near.

Do you know people like that?

After five months

So that's it.
Five months later.
I told you that I can't be friends with you.
That I can't be a part of your life anymore.
It's sounds so easy after all your hurtings.
But it hurts. I miss you. Sometimes just a little, sometimes as much that my heart feels so heavy like a stone.
It breaks me that you are not fine with yourself.
That you are sad.
I wish I could be the one to show you strength and the lights in your life.
I wish you would have fought for my presence in your life.
Giving you back your things NOW hurts me more than giving them to you five months ago.
I know it's not our last word. It hurts to know that Saturday we will go our seperate ways without eachother again.
A fixed date when it'll hurt a little more again.
Maybe just for a little while.
We don't love eachother anymore,
but it makes me still sad anyway.

What is one thing you still didn't gave them back?

Herzensmensch

Es sind die Menschen die dich verletzen und du sie trotzdem
nicht hassen kannst.
Ich versuche Dinge zu finden die mich an dir stören.
Ich finde kaum etwas.
Es sind die Menschen dessen Gegenwart Abdrücke auf deinem
Herzen hinterlassen.
Die Menschen die du ewig nicht gesehen hast und davon aus-
gehst sie gehören zu einem anderen Lebensabschnitt.
Die, bei denen du beim zufälligen wiedersehen feststellst, das
sie dir doch gefehlt haben.
Die, die dich gutes und schlechtes fühlen lassen.
Die, die dich über die Liebe lehren.
Diese Menschen die dich wachsen lassen und trotz Streit immer
da sein werden.

Du fühlst dich an wie einer dieser Herzensmenschen. Ich
glaube ich bin einer deiner Herzensmenschen, auch wenn du
es vielleicht gar nicht weißt.

It's the people who hurt you and you can't hate them.

I'm trying to find things that bother me about you. I can't finde those.

It is the people whose presence leaves imprints on your heart.

The people you don't see forever and you assume to not care.

The ones you realise when you see each other again that you missed them.

The ones that make you feel good and bad.

Those who teach you about love.

Those people who let you grow and will always be there despite quarrels.

You feel like one of those people of the heart, even if it might not be true. And I feel like I am yours, even if you don't know it.

Him and I

He looked at me, like there is still something in me,
worth looking at.

He was my warmth.
I was his peace.

He was my art.
Where the world had left him grey,
I had the colors to paint.

In so many bad eyes,
I saw the good ones
with these angel eyes.

I made mistakes and
you do either.

You were there, looked at me.
Looked at me like I was your definition of a unique wonder.
Of a wholesome, healing love.

I wish we could just protect us from everything that hurts.

What is worth from yourself?

I was sure.

I was sure that, I found my love in 2021.
            my type was bruenette.
            my first kiss was the best.
            I loved this boy from my past.

But then a light, brighter than the stars.
                warmer than the sun.
                 prettier than the nightsky.
                more colorfull than every sunset.
Our first look, like a fairytale.
Our first touch, like a storm
Our first kiss, like a never ending happiness
Our break up, like the worst thing that my heart ever felt.

And the shock, I can´t hate you.
            you are still amazing.

After all the lies, I am so hurt. But I simply can´t hate you for
that.

Why?
        We are young, we can´t be perfect, nobody is. We need
to get hurt, to fall down and stand up again.. And that is okay.

So this is what I learned from you. I wasn´t sure in 2021, I was
wrong because you were my first love in 2022. You were my
sun.

What do you learn, what your younger self didn´t knew about yourself?

75

You never knew it…

…that you were my role model,
that I thought I communicate so much and you nothing at all
and that I was sure, that I showed you everyday
how much I loved you.

Yesterday you told me that you doesn´t felt it that way.
I am still shocked, because for me it was the exact opposite.
I know I made mistakes too,
but it hurt me that you saw it that way.

But then the next moment you said that you admired me and
that I was perfect in your eyes and still be perfect.

But why do we write that way when we go seperate ways from
Saturday on.

And again…

There is still something between us,
a spark, a feeling in the stomach,
but we let our heads stop our hearts from moving and loving.

Who is your role model? Say them that they are your role model.

Who is your role model? Say them that they are your role model.

I wish I was healed when I met you

But would´ve helped us? – Maybe.
But the point is that your love healed, me step by step,
                                            , piece by piece.

I was so suspicious about the fact that you really wanted me,
that I built up walls there should have been doors.
Kept my heart guarded, afraid oft he wars that love had waged
on me before.

Yet you stayed. Softended the edges of my fear, turned doubt
into something dear.
And for a while, I thought love could fix everything.

But maybe our love for eachother alone was not enough for the
moment..
Maybe healing isn´t just about holding on,
but knowing when to let go.

So here we are- not broken
                not whole.
Just two teenagers who loved, but couldn´t stay.

Circle the five most powerful words in the poem.

Your company and our foodsteps

I liked being alone
but that is the reason why I knew
that you was different.

Because for the first time ever,
I wanted someone else's company
more than my own.

You changed me.
In every respect.
With every touch and every word.

Your foodsteps and my foodsteps,
engraved side by side,
at the same place of my heart.

Highlight your favorite word and use it in a different sentence.

81

All of the maybes.

Maybe we needed to learn to let
our love fade away.
I don´t say that it was easy,
but I think it was important.

Important for our self respect.
We learnd a lot about letting someone go
and hold them near anyways.

And I know we will never be 100% separated.

Do we really miss forever?

I will forever miss the way,

we kissed when we were kids.
I miss your touch, your lips and the way we lived.

It was my first relationship.
I was not that much experienced.
With you I experienced joy and pain,
through every storm and trough the rain.

The path ahead may still be wide,
but in my heart, I've come to guide.
The inner compass, strong and true,
the journey's more than just the view.

What symbolizes a „promise ring" for you?

Missing promise ring

I found the box in my closet with all of your things you left. Filled with pieces of you, of us, left untouched since the day we fell apart.

Fingertips tracing memories, hearts stitched into letters, whispers folded between the lines.
I searched fort he box with our promise ring, the silent vow we once believed in.

And it hurtss, not knowing where it is, or if it simply slipped away, like we did.

How would you name this power of breaking hearts?

Hurt enough hearts

I hurt so many hearts
Just because you one hurt mine.

I just hurt them before they have the chance to hurt me.

I doesn´t wanna hurt more hearts,
I wanna heal the ones I break.
And maybe that´s the point,
I wanna make people feel good
Meanwhile you hurt people over and over again.

You are not a bad person, but I think that you doesn´t notice
how your acts make people feel sometimes.

So it is true,
Hurt people hurt people.

How does this attraction feels to you?

89

Irrestistible Pull

I knew why we couldn't be friends.
I could suddenly be strict and tell you that I can't stay as a friend.
It is our attraction. Stronger than any will and irrestistible. A drug for the soul. Like a vortex from which you want to swim away but the current is too strong and you are always ground back.

But maybe it is just that this attraction won't work for us as long as we have contact. An attraction that can not be more than friendship and is too strong for a friendship.

What is something you can only feel in silence?

91

A touch of silence

Your name lingers like an echo in my bones,
soft as a whisper, loud as a storm.
Between the lines of silence,
I hear you still, a love unspoken,
yet never still.

Our spark
One glance
And the air
Catches fire again

I have to admit one thing.
I have never let anyone
get so close to me again,
after you.

But why doesn´t exist a thing between beeing friend and beeing in love with someone?

93

I cannot be your friend.

I might be able to if we were just friends from the beginning.
But I feel this connection&attraction and I am direclty more into
it,
when we write only for a day,
that I sould.

But why feels missing you like that?

What was the reason why love wasn't enough?

95

Isn´t it enough?

Isn´t it enough that you get always the best out of me and I get
the best out of you?
Isn´t it enough that our attraction after everything that has hap-
pend is still as permanent as something unconditional?

Write down for what you are looking.

I do not know

I don´t know if it is love i am looking for or just a person who
feels like you.

But please do not be able to hurt me again.
My heart loves and hates
to be in love with a piece of you.

It hurts and it heals.
It is like rain and rainbows.
Like darkness and sunlight.
Like coldness and warmth.

Lessons and learnings.

Why do you do not revenge them?

No revenge because…
I wrote over a whole book about us.
I found my healing and confidence in writing poetry.
I put all my love for you in words and chosse to heal and not to hurt.

Do you know a reason why someone is not able to be honest with the turth of their feelings?

Not able

But why I am not able to tell you the truth?
I am scared of your reaction and my hurt.
And maybe this is the answer that makes me understand why
You were not able to be honestly with me.

Write a message for their birthday with all the things you still feel behind the „happy birthday".

Do you mind that I am not there?
I would like to be more than just a message.
We are no longer the same and we both know that.
But on days like these, I regret deleting our playlist.
On days like these, I want to embrace you.
On days like these, I want to hear you laugh and make you happy.
But the only thing that left to say is:
„happy birthday“

How would you discribe or draw the space you met them?

105

How would you discribe or draw the space you met them?

Half-light

We met,
we met in the space between songs,
where silence
felt like a nostalgic language,
that only we could speak.

What is something you are afraid of?

Afraid

I am afraid that someone won´t fall in love with me again.

No…

I am afraid that I can´t fall in love again.

Draw a picture about this poem.

Untaken Jump

If one of them would jump in the ocean,
the other one wouldn´t be that afraid of the step.
If both jump, they would be together again.
But they don´t.
The scary thoughts inside their heads,
the „what if-questions"
about their feelings for each other,
don´t let them take the risk.

What do you understand under the „Ex-effect"?

„The Ex-Effect"

You miss me now that I´ve moved on,
a ghost you swore was long since gone.
You give me hope,
then slowly fade away.
Say „this won´t work",
act like you are fine and do not care.
While I still ache like you were mine.

What is your own character trait about yourself?

Your best character trait

The best trait about you were, that you were always able to
make me smile.
When I was sad- you maked me happy.
When I felt alone-you gave me a home.
Even at the day we met for clarity,
you told me that your only goal was to make me smile again.
And I think that is still the best part of you.
That even if our world was about to end,
you made me smile for a second.

Write something about your favorite line of „Familiar strangers".

115

We weren´t just love,
we were warmth on cold nights,
a lifeline when the world felt too heavy.
We carried each other trough storms,
built a home in whispered words and steady hands.

At some point, the fire softened.
Love became less about heartbeats and more about eartache.
And when silence grew louder than our laughter,
we let go.

For a while, it got easier.
I learned to live without your name echoing in my mind.
But then, a message-
A few words, a familiar rhythm
and suddenly, I was drowning in you again.

How can something feel so distant,
yet so close it steals my breath?
Maybe love never leaves,
maybe it just waits.
Waits somewhere between the lines of a song.

Have you ever experienced someone turning from „home" to a „stranger"?

Between the lines

We talk in words that dance like fire,
soft and bright, yet full of mire.
He says the things I long to hear,
but do they mean what they appear?

I wonder if he sees my mind,
or just the frame that lies outside.
And if he prays when no one´s near.
Is faith in him, or just my fear?

What do you think is really mean with „between the lines"?
Write a secret message you wish someone would read between your
lines.

Half-written

And I, I stood still.
Because maybe for the first time
after the heartbreaks I never posted,
after the almosts that never hurt enough,
you felt like a „maybe"
turning into a chance.

But maybe you are not mine to keep.
Just another poem, half written,
on a screen I'll keep opening
and closing again.

Finish the poem. What happens next? Write a last verse or a continuation.

121

The shimmer in my eyes

And maybe that shimmer stays in my eyes
everytime I speak of you.
And maybe the box in my closet
will remain like a souvenir of forever.
Because everytime you leave,
I forget what it´s like when you are here.

I am afraid of love.
Just not yours.

I promise, I tried to let go of you, honestly.
But my heart holds onto memories,
like children holds promises.

And every „It is better this way",
sounded quieter than what we once were.
I can´t forget what never really said „goodbye".
Because you stayed,
between the lines in the songs
and in the echo of a smile,
only you knew.

What is a memory you can't let go of, even if it's silent now?

I feel used.

My friend are saying I have a „flirty character".
He only wants my body.
And you?
My body is the only thing that still impress you.
The only thing from me you want.
And all that because I have a „flirty character"?

Write a letter to yourself reminding you that your worth goes far beyond what others see or want from you.

Lover girl

I wanna be a lover girl again.
I want to be loved und I want to love again.
I want the hugs and the feeling of beeing home again.
I hate to do not have him when I am not the best version of me.
I growth so much and I know that I am strong,
but inside me is still a girl who just wants to have arms to go
back through.
And instead of searching other arms I hold on to yours.
I just want this one special kind of hug.
The hug without a limit.
The strong hug that warms your heart and makes you feel free
again.

<3

Describe or draw the kind of hug that feels like home.

I was sure

I was sure that I found my love in 2021,
　　　　　that my type was brunette,
　　　　　that my first kiss was the best and
　　　　　that I loved that boy.
But then a light, brighter than the stars,
　　　　　　　warmer than the sun and
　　　　　　　prettier than the night lights,
Our first look, like a fairytale.
Our first touch, like a storm in my heart.
Our first kiss, like a never ending happiness.
Our break up,
　　　　　like the worst thing that I felt as far.

And the shock, I can`t hate you.
You are amazing.
After all the lies, after all the hurtings,
I am not able to hate you.

Why?
　　　We are young, we are not perfect,
　　　we have to hurt, to fall down and to learn.
　　　And THATS OKAY.

So that's what I learned,
I was not sure in 2021 because the first real love…that was you.

What did you think was „forever" once- and what did you learn
from letting go of it?

You never knew it

That you were my role model.
That I thought I communicate so much and you nothing at all.
That I was sure, that I showed you everyday how much I loved
you.

Yesterday you told me that you doesn't felt it that way.
I am still sad..because for me it was the opposite.
I know I made mistakes too,
but it hurted me that you saw it that way.

The next moment you said that you admired me and that I was
perfect in your eyes and still be perfect.

But why do we write that way when weg o sepparate ways
from Saturday on?

And again. There is still something between us, a spark, a fee-
ling in my stomach, to little to find a definition for it, so we le
tour heads stop our hearts from loving one another.

Write a message you never sent. Let the unsaid things find their place here.

Wish I was healed when I met you.

But would´ve helped us? – Maybe.
But the point is that your love healed me, step by step,
                              breath by breath,
                              piece by piece.
I was so suspicious about the fact that you really wanted me,
that I built up walls where should have been doors.
Kept in my heart guarded, afraid ot the wars that love had wa-
ged before.

Yet you stayed. Softended the edges of my fear, turned doubt
into something clear.
And for a while, I thought love could fix everything.

But maybe love alone was never enough.
Maybe healing is not just about holding on,
but knowing when to let go.

So here we are, not broken,
                    not whole,
just two teenagers who loved, but couldn´t stay.

Circle the five most powerful words in the poem an use each of them in your own sentence or short poem.

Your company and our foodsteps

I liked being alone.

But that is why I knew you were different,
because fort he first time ever I wanted someone elses company
more than just my own.

You changed me.
In every respect.

With every touch and every word.

Your foodsteps, my foodsteps,
engraved side by side,
at the same place of my heart.

*Write about a person who changed the way you feel about being a-
lone.*

I needed to lose you to love me

Yes, I learned to stand alone
But now we the love tries to find me,
I flinch, I smile, then shut the door.
Because somewhere along healing I stopped believing,
that love could stay without breaking me.

What did losing someone teach you about loving yourself?
Write a letter to your future self.

137

We´ve all been there-

The first big fight, the one that felt like the end.
I thought the same.

You replayed every word, every look,
like it could fix something.
I`ve tried that too.

I don´t even remember what started it.
Funny how it all seemed so big.

But now?
It´s something that is still there,
but no longer what it was.

Now it is just silence where a person used to be.

What seemed huge back then but feels small now?
Reflect on what really mattered.

Our somewhere only we know is our old Dance school,
where our eyes met for the first time.
It is the stair in our school where we sat in our breaks.
The bus seats where I still see a telegram of you, of us.
The bank where we became a couple and
the film after that we kissed for the first time.
And the place where we saw a rainbow at our first date.

So I think our „somewhere only we know" is not only a place,
it is a feeling we had there.

Describe your own „somewhere only we know"- a place or feeling that holds memory only you and that one special person under-stand.

It is difficult.

It is so difficult to wait,
but more difficult to regret.
But why?

What do you think „why“?
Do you regret more what you did or what you didn´t do?
Write about a moment you still think about.

Childhood shelter

My childhood shelter
You held the world
Like it couldn´t break us,
built caves from blankets,
called fear by name
and stayed anyway.
I learned from you, that being soft,
can also be strong.

Who made you feel safe as a child?
Write them a thank you.

What if...?

But what if I loose you forever this way ?
Maybe I want to find an other way than Conan Gray.
Yes I can´t be your friend,
can´t be your lover,
can´t be the reason we hold back eachother from falling in love
with somebody other than me…
but maybe I can make it feel okay for the moment.

*Write about a time you had to choose between holding on and let-
ting go.*

Day 268 after our Break Up

Some days are easy,

                    maybe to easy.

Some days are hard,

                    maybe to hard.

I hate that healing and moving on from you isn't linear.

When I catch a glimpse of us again…

                              you get cold.

But when you catch a spark of it again…

                                  I get warm.

It hurts not beeing able to move on completly.

And I am so angry that being without me is so easy for you.

Describe a day from your healing journey- what did it teach you about yourself?

It was supposed to be you.

Supposed to bring our kids to bed,
to hold me warm when I get cold.
To laugh at burned toast on Sunday mornings,
to fight over silly things
and make up before the day ends.

It was supposed to be you, waiting at the door when I'd come
home late,
learning how to fold my silence into something soft.

You-
        the one who knew my worst and still stayed.
The one who'd grow old next to my bones,
still seeing me like that very first day.

But it wasn't.
And now I make the bed alone,
talkt o shadows where you should be,
and smile at a future that never learned your name written next
to mine.

What dream or future once felt real, but never happened?
Write your little goodbye to it.

Getting rid of him was one of the hardest things I ever had to do.

Not because I am not able to live without him,
but because I had imagined every version of my life
with him in it.

I had to unlearn the soundso f his name on ordinary days,
had to teach my hands to stop reaching for what no longer
reached back.

It wasn't just the fact that I needed to let go of him as a person.
It was a letting go of promises,
of weekend mornings that never came
and the fact I will not take his last name one day.

And still,
some nights I miss him,
with a softness that feels almost like love.

But I don't look back anymore.
Only forward.
Even if some parts of me still carry his echo.

What's something that hurt but you're proud you did?

All of the lana del ray songs,

…that replay in my head everytime I think of you.
Sometimes when I close my eyes,
I think about random moments with you.
The way I looked at you in the car or
the way you touched my chin.

And I hate the way I think of you and
the way you maked me smile even when I cried.
The way you hurted me and left me with no lies.
And sometimes I hate that you didn't cheated because
how do you let go of someone who were good to you most of
the time?

Choose a song that reminds you of a person or a memory.
Why?

No revenge because you told me about your mom.
About how unloved you felt and how I gave you the feeling of being able to accept that true, unconditional love exists. Not because we shared the same blood, because the connection that touched our hearts was like a strong glow stick. But even glowsticks needs to be broken before they glow as pretty as they do.

Write about a moment where you chose healing instead of hurting them back. What helped you decide?

I am the poet.

So yes, I am the poet.
And yes, that whole book is full with my feelings and thoughts
all packed in lines.
So everyone is able to admire the poems,
but who pauses to understand the poet?

n

Write a note to someone you wish really saw you.

You weren't just another chapter.
You were the whole book,
but you dropped the pen
when the plot got too real.

And I kept waiting…
Waiting for the next sentence-
not knowing,
you'd already closed the app.

Who never gave you a ending?

There were marthas.

…and maybe they were good for him-
gentle, steady, safe.

But I, I was his Allie.
Not because I was his chaos,
but because I was his „once in a lifetime."

Not the loudest,
not the easiest,
but the one he never really let go of.

The one who stayed,
even when she left.

But what is better for you?

I miss him, but I can´t tell him…

One year after this heartbreak I realised that

I told it hundred of other hearts. Maybe he will read this book

filled with all of the hurt, the emotions and the love.

I will never forget him and I will never forget this journey.

Even if it hurted me like nothing else, it was good that it hap-

pend. I thank you for beeing a part of my journey and I thank

him for building a part of me I am grown in.

He was not just my first relationship, he was my everyting.

Once in a while I saw that something in his eyes and I think

what should be, will be. So maybe we will see each other again

filled with love and pureness in our eyes, maybe.

Without this hurt and all of the highs and lows, I wouldn´t have

wrote a whole book filled with the journey of healing after him.

And yes, I never thought that there would be a after him, but

here it is and I am in it and fort he moment, I am fine with this.

Thank you for beeing so much more than just a boy for me.

Nobody knew about this book project of me but with the pub-

lishing of this book they are able to know about all this, he is

able to know about this process and thats okay for me because

it is a part of me. I thank all my followers on my account

„silentwhisperofme". You are a part of my journey. And just

because I finish this book now, doen´t mean the healing process

and journey are finished. Thank you.